BE GOOD
TO-YOURSELF
THERAPY

BE-GOOD-TO-YOURSELF THERAPY

WRITTEN BY CHERRY HARTMAN

ILLUSTRATED BY R. W. ALLEY

An Abbey Press Book

WARNER BOOKS

A Time Warner Company

An Abbey Press Book

Warner Books Edition
Copyright © 1987 St. Meinrad Archabbey
All rights reserved.

This Warner Books edition is published by arrangement with Abbey Press, St. Meinrad, Indiana

Warner Books, Inc. 1271 Avenue of the Americas, New York, NY 10020

 A Time Warner Company

Printed in the United States of America

First Warner Books Printing: December 1992

10 9 8 7 6 5 4

Library of Congress Cataloging in Publication Data
Hartman, Cherry
   Be-good-to-yourself therapy / Cherry Hartman : Illustrations by
R.W. Alley. -- Warner Books ed.
      p.   cm.
   Originally published : St. Meinrad, Ind. : Abbey Press, c1987.
   "An Abbey Press book."
   ISBN 0-446-39394-0
   1. Self-actualization (Psychology)   I. Title.
BF637.S4H36   1992
158' . 1--dc20   92-28817
                                                                      CIP

Cover design by Julia Kushnirsky

Foreword

In the course of growing up, many folks pick up attitudes that drag them down. Do you feel bad if you express anger? Are you ashamed by your feelings? Do you harass yourself if you make a mistake or fail? Do you experience guilt when you put your own needs before those of others? <u>Be-good-to-yourself Therapy</u> was written to help you overcome the distorted notions that keep you from living fully and honestly.

Although many people today may equate self-esteem with self-indulgence, genuine self-love begins with the recognition that each of us is God's handiwork. To love oneself is to express love for God, the Creator. What's more, you cannot be a gift to others unless you nurture your own spiritual, psychological, and physical well-being.

In this booklet, Cherry Hartman, a clinical social worker for over sixteen years, has compiled basic rules for coping from day to day. Be good to yourself—enjoy this book and let its rules free you for more peaceful, harmonious living.

1.

Trust yourself. You know what you want and need.

2.

Put yourself first. You can't
be anything for anybody else
unless you take care of yourself.

3.

Let your feelings be known.
They are important.

4.

Express your opinions.
It's good to hear yourself talk.

5.

Value your thinking.
You do it well.

6.

Take the time and space
you need—even if other people
are wanting something from you.

7.

When you need something,
don't talk yourself out of it.
Even if you can't have it,
it's OK to need.

8.

When you're scared,
let someone know. Isolating
yourself when you're scared
makes it worse.

9.

When you feel like running away, let yourself feel the scare. Think about what you fear will happen and decide what you need to do.

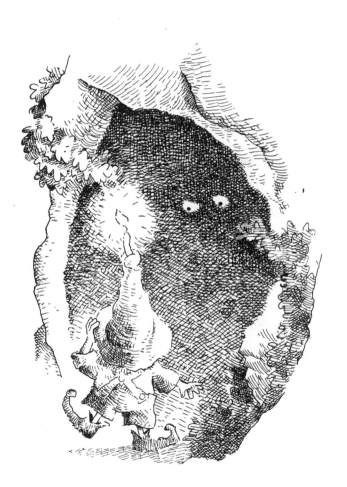

10.

When you're angry, let yourself
feel the anger. Decide what you
want to do: just feel it,
express it, or take some action.

_11._

When you're sad, think about
what would be comforting.

12.

When you're hurt, tell the person who hurt you. Keeping it inside makes it grow.

13.

When you see someone else's hurt face, breathe. You are not responsible for making other people happy.

14.

When you have work to do and you don't want to do it, decide what really needs to be done and what can wait.

15.

When you want something from someone else, ask. You'll be OK if they say no. Asking is being true to yourself.

16.

When you need help, ask.
Trust people to say no if they
don't want to give.

17.

When people turn you down,
it usually has to do with them
and not with you. Ask someone
else for what you need.

18.

When you feel alone, know there
are people who want to be with you.
Fantasize what it would be like
to be with each of them. Decide
if you want to make that happen.

19.

When you feel anxious,
let yourself know that in your
head you've moved into the future
to something scary and your body
has gotten up the energy for it.
Come back to the present.

20.

When you want to say something loving to someone, go ahead. Expressing your feelings is not a commitment.

21.

When someone yells at you, physically support yourself by relaxing into your chair or putting your feet firmly on the floor. Remember to breathe. Think about the message they are trying to get across to you.

22.

When you're harassing yourself, stop. You do it when you need something. Figure out what you need and get it.

23.

When everything seems wrong,
you are overwhelmed and need some
comforting. Ask for it.
Afterwards, you can think about
what you need to do.

24.

When you want to talk to someone new and are scared, breathe. Don't start rehearsing, just plunge in. If it doesn't go well, you can stop.

25.

If you're doing something you don't like to do (such as smoking or overeating), stop. Think about what you really want. If you're stuck and can't think clearly, talk out loud to someone.

26.

When you can't think straight,
stop thinking. Feel.

27.

When you're in need of love,
reach out. There are people
who love you.

28.

When you're confused, it's usually because you think you should do one thing and you want to do another. Dialogue with yourself out loud or on paper, or present both sides to a friend.

29.

When you feel harried, slow down. Deliberately slow your breathing, your speech, and your movements.

30.

When you have tears, cry.

31.

When you feel like crying and
it's not a safe place to cry,
acknowledge your pain and promise
yourself a good cry later.
Keep your promise.

32.

When somebody does you wrong,
be actively angry with them.

33.

When everything seems gray,
look for color.

34.

When you feel like a baby,
take care of the baby in you.

35.

When somebody gives you a gift,
say "thank you." That's all
you need to do. A gift is not
an obligation.

36.

When somebody loves you, just accept and be glad. Love is not an obligation. You don't have to do anything in return.

37.

If one of these rules seems wrong for you, talk about it with someone. Then, rewrite it so it fits for you.

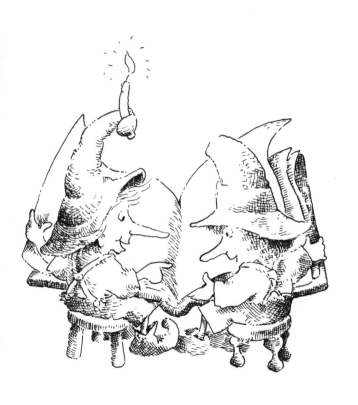